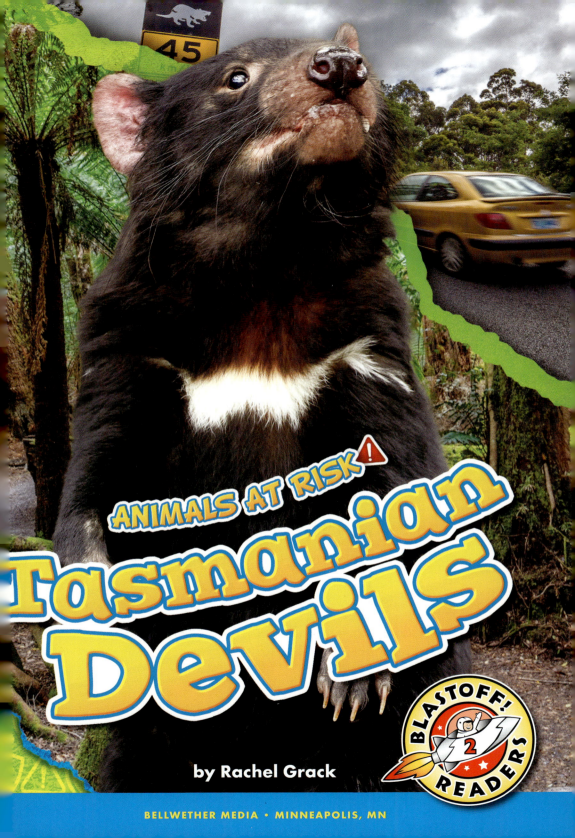

ANIMALS AT RISK

Tasmanian Devils

by Rachel Grack

BLASTOFF! READERS

BELLWETHER MEDIA • MINNEAPOLIS, MN

Blastoff! Readers are carefully developed by literacy experts to build reading stamina and move students toward fluency by combining standards-based content with developmentally appropriate text.

Level 1 provides the most support through repetition of high-frequency words, light text, predictable sentence patterns, and strong visual support.

Level 2 offers early readers a bit more challenge through varied sentences, increased text load, and text-supportive special features.

Level 3 advances early-fluent readers toward fluency through increased text load, less reliance on photos, advancing concepts, longer sentences, and more complex special features.

★ **Blastoff! Universe**

 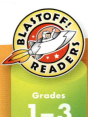 

This edition first published in 2023 by Bellwether Media, Inc.

No part of this publication may be reproduced in whole or in part without written permission of the publisher. For information regarding permission, write to Bellwether Media, Inc., Attention: Permissions Department, 6012 Blue Circle Drive, Minnetonka, MN 55343.

Library of Congress Cataloging-in-Publication Data

Names: Koestler-Grack, Rachel A., 1973- author.
Title: Tasmanian devils / by Rachel Grack.
Description: Minneapolis, MN : Bellwether Media, Inc., 2023. | Series: Blastoff! Readers. Animals at Risk | Includes bibliographical references and index. | Audience: Ages 5-8 | Audience: Grades 2-3 | Summary: "Relevant images match informative text in this introduction to Tasmanian devils. Intended for students in kindergarten through third grade"-- Provided by publisher.
Identifiers: LCCN 2022037561 (print) | LCCN 2022037562 (ebook) | ISBN 9798886871210 (library binding) | ISBN 9798886872477 (ebook)
Subjects: LCSH: Tasmanian devil--Juvenile literature. | Endangered species--Juvenile literature.
Classification: LCC QL737.M33 K64 2023 (print) | LCC QL737.M33 (ebook) | DDC 599.2/7--dc23/eng/20220811
LC record available at https://lccn.loc.gov/2022037561
LC ebook record available at https://lccn.loc.gov/2022037562

Text copyright © 2023 by Bellwether Media, Inc. BLASTOFF! READERS and associated logos are trademarks and/or registered trademarks of Bellwether Media, Inc.

Editor: Kieran Downs   Designer: Brittany McIntosh

Printed in the United States of America, North Mankato, MN.

Table of Contents

Feisty Animals 4
In Danger! 8
Save the Tasmanian Devils! 12
Glossary 22
To Learn More 23
Index 24

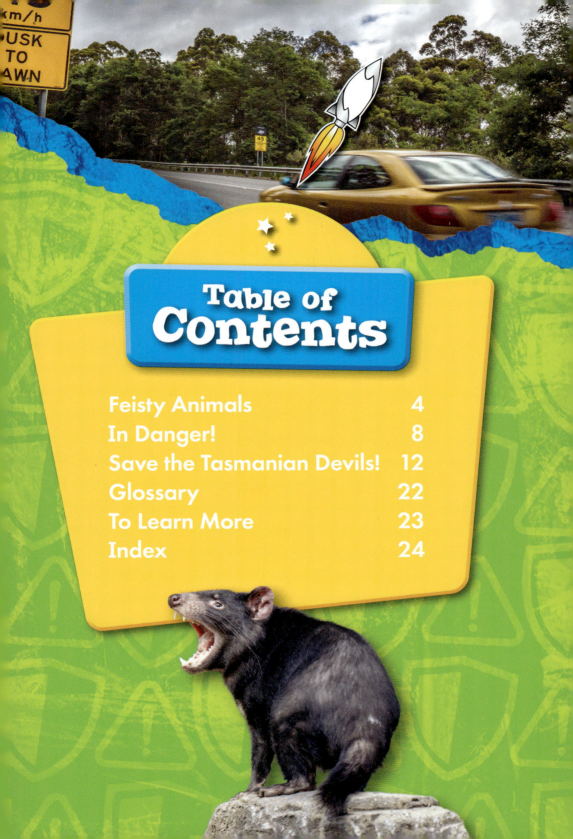

Feisty Animals

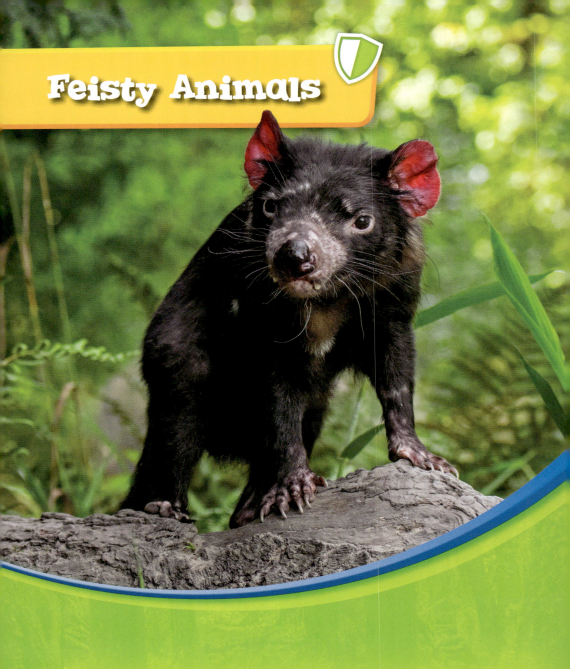

Tasmanian devils are **marsupials**. Their fur is mostly black. They are mean and **feisty**!

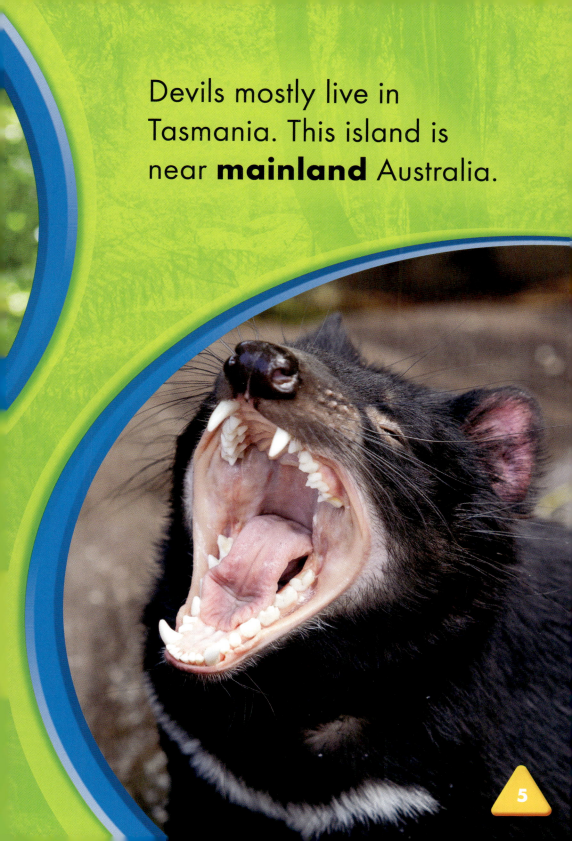

Devils mostly live in Tasmania. This island is near **mainland** Australia.

Devils once lived across Australia. They are now **endangered**.

People and **disease** have caused most of their troubles.

Tasmanian Devil Range

range =

In Danger!

farmland

People clear Tasmania's land for farms. Devils lose their homes.

Farmers see devils as pests. They kill them. Many devils also get hit by cars.

Threats

1 people clear land

2 people make farms

3 devils lose their homes

Disease spreads easily among devils. Large **tumors** grow around their mouths.

The lumps make eating hard. Devils quickly **starve**.

tumor

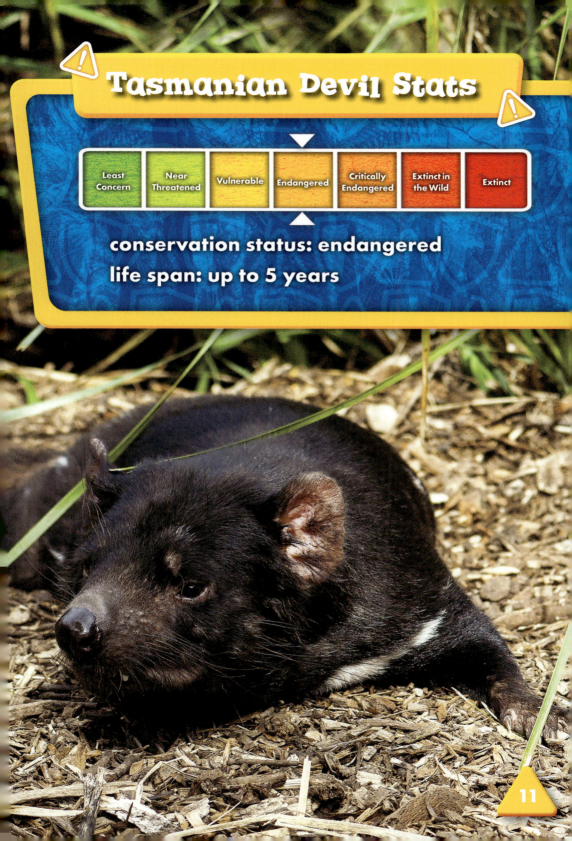

Tasmanian Devil Stats

| Least Concern | Near Threatened | Vulnerable | Endangered | Critically Endangered | Extinct in the Wild | Extinct |

conservation status: endangered

life span: up to 5 years

Save the Tasmanian Devils!

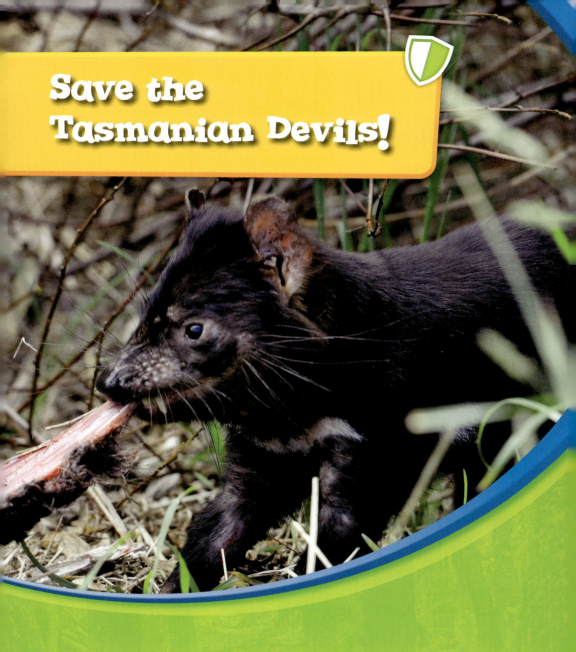

Tasmanian devils keep their homes healthy. These **scavengers** eat dead animals.

They are also top **predators**. They keep **prey** numbers healthy.

The World with Tasmanian Devils

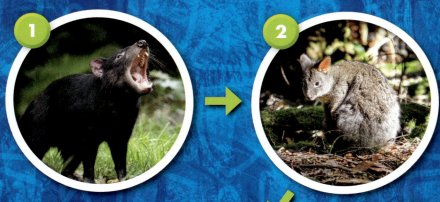

1. more devils
2. healthy wildlife

3. healthy homes

Tasmania set up **reserves** for devils. People cannot farm on this land.

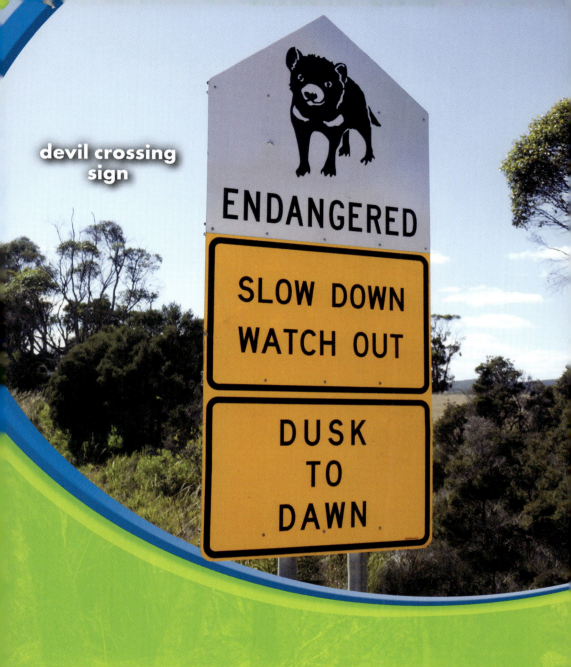

devil crossing sign

Safe driving also saves devils. Drivers slow down around wildlife.

wildlife workers studying a devil

Wildlife workers help sick devils. They test new **treatments**.

They try to slow the spread of sickness in the wild.

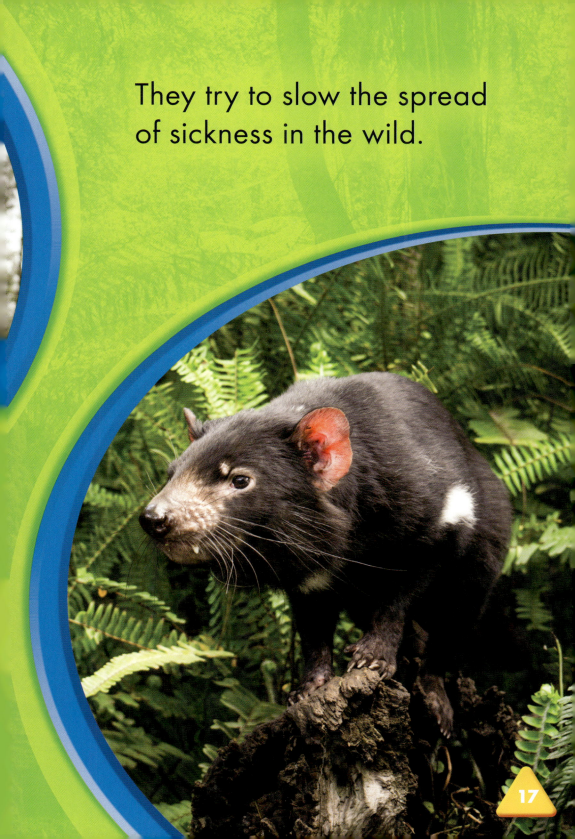

Devils are returning to Australia. Some live in mainland reserves.

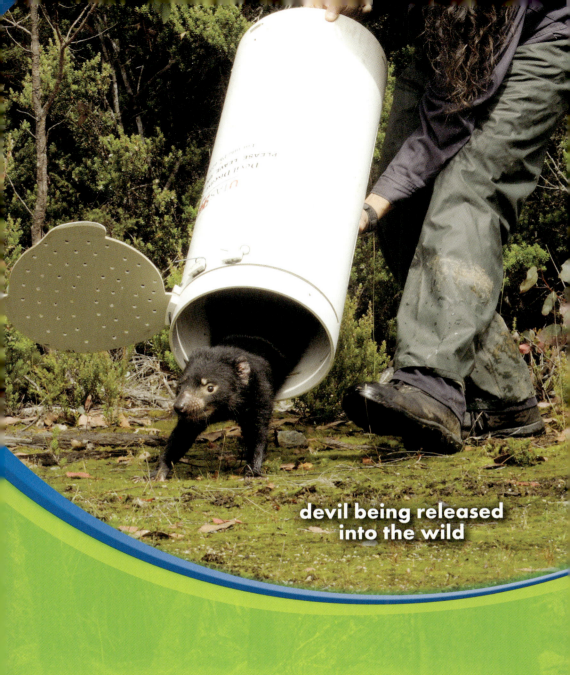

devil being released into the wild

These devils stay safe and healthy. Their numbers are growing.

Anyone can help save Tasmanian devils. They can teach others about devils.

They can **donate** money to wildlife groups. These acts keep devils around!

Glossary

disease—sickness

donate—to give gifts, mostly money

endangered—in danger of dying out

feisty—easily angered or likely to fight

mainland—a continent or main part of a continent

marsupials—a group of animals that includes kangaroos, koalas, and opossums; female marsupials carry their young in pouches at their stomachs.

predators—animals that hunt other animals for food

prey—animals that are hunted by other animals for food

reserves—areas of land set aside for wild animals

scavengers—animals that eat dead animals for food

starve—to go without food and die of hunger

treatments—ways of caring for a sick animal

tumors—lumps caused by a sickness

To Learn More

AT THE LIBRARY

Arnold, Quinn M. *Tasmanian Devils*. Mankato, Minn.: Creative Education, 2020.

Grack, Rachel. *Black-footed Ferrets*. Minneapolis, Minn.: Bellwether Media, 2023.

Klepinger, Teresa. *Wolverine vs. Tasmanian Devil*. Minneapolis, Minn.: Kaleidoscope, 2022.

ON THE WEB

FACTSURFER

Factsurfer.com gives you a safe, fun way to find more information.

1. Go to www.factsurfer.com.

2. Enter "Tasmanian devils" into the search box and click 🔍.

3. Select your book cover to see a list of related content.

Index

Australia, 5, 6, 18
cars, 9
color, 4
disease, 7, 10
donate, 20
driving, 15
endangered, 6
farms, 8, 9, 14
fur, 4
homes, 8, 12
marsupials, 4
numbers, 19
people, 7, 8, 14
predators, 13
prey, 13
range, 7
reserves, 14, 18
scavengers, 12
sickness, 16, 17
stats, 11
Tasmania, 5, 8, 14
threats, 9
treatments, 16
tumors, 10
ways to help, 20
wild, 17, 19
wildlife workers, 16, 20
world with, 13

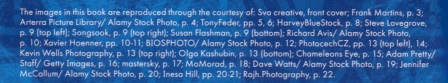

The images in this book are reproduced through the courtesy of: Sva creative, front cover; Frank Martins, p. 3; Arterra Picture Library/ Alamy Stock Photo, p. 4; TonyFeder, pp. 5, 6; HarveyBlueStock, p. 8; Steve Lovegrove, p. 9 (top left); Songsook, p. 9 (top right); Susan Flashman, p. 9 (bottom); Richard Avis/ Alamy Stock Photo, p. 10; Xavier Hoenner, pp. 10-11; BIOSPHOTO/ Alamy Stock Photo, p. 12; PhotocechCZ, pp. 13 (top left), 14; Kevin Wells Photography, p. 13 (top right); Olga Kashubin, p. 13 (bottom); Chameleons Eye, p. 15; Adam Pretty/ Staff/ Getty Images, p. 16; mastersky, p. 17; MoMorad, p. 18; Dave Watts/ Alamy Stock Photo, p. 19; Jennifer McCallum/ Alamy Stock Photo, p. 20; Inesa Hill, pp. 20-21; Rajh.Photography, p. 22.